Sports Illustrated KIDS

SOCCER'S Most CONTROVERSIAL PLAYS

YOU MAKE the CALL!

by Heather E. Schwartz

CAPSTONE PRESS
a capstone imprint

Published by Capstone Press, an imprint of Capstone
1710 Roe Crest Drive, North Mankato, Minnesota 56003
capstonepub.com

Library of Congress Cataloging-in-Publication Data
is available on the Library of Congress website.
ISBN: 9798875257537 (hardcover)
ISBN: 9798875257483 (paperback)
ISBN: 9798875257490 (ebook PDF)

Summary: The refs made their calls on three controversial soccer plays. Take a closer look at each play and make your own call.

Editorial Credits
Editor: Christianne Jones; Designer: Tracy Davies; Media Researcher: Svetlana Zhurkin; Production Specialist: Whitney Shaefer

Image Credits
Associated Press: 21; Getty Images: Allsport, 20, Allsport/Mike King, 22, Archivo El Grafico, 19, Bongarts/Stuart Franklin, 9, Buda Mendes, 6, Cameron Spencer, 14, Clive Rose, 15, Franklin Jacome, 29 (left), Joern Pollex, 13, Kevin C. Cox, 8, Michael Steele, 12, 16, Pool/José Jácome, 10, Wagner Meier, 11; Newscom: Sipa USA/Bildbyran/Mathias Bergeld, 25, Sipa USA/SPP/Noe Llamas, 27, ZUMA Press/Bildbyran/Mathias Bergeld, 24, ZUMA Press/DDP/Star-Images, 7, ZUMA Press/Ira L. Black, 26, ZUMA Press/Scott Coleman, 5; Shutterstock: Andrey Burmakin, cover (bottom), Lana Sham, back cover, 17, 23, 28, 29 (right), Muhammad Muhdi (dotted background), cover (top) and throughout

Words in **BOLD** can be found in the glossary.

Printed and bound in China. PO 6459

TABLE OF CONTENTS

UP FOR DEBATE

Pro soccer players race up and down the pitch, putting their skills to the test. They battle for control of the ball. Goalkeepers do their best to **thwart** the other team's efforts. As time ends, only one team can come out the winner. The team that plays the best deserves a well-earned victory.

Professional soccer is more than a pastime. It is a game **regulated** by rules that are **enforced** by officials. They are part of what makes the game interesting to watch, even when calls are controversial.

THE RULES HOLD PLAYERS TO A STANDARD THAT KEEPS PLAY SAFE AND FAIR.

And the truth is, not everyone agrees when officials make their final decisions.

SOME CALLS ARE SO CONTROVERSIAL, SOCCER FANS CONTINUE DEBATING THEM FOR DECADES!

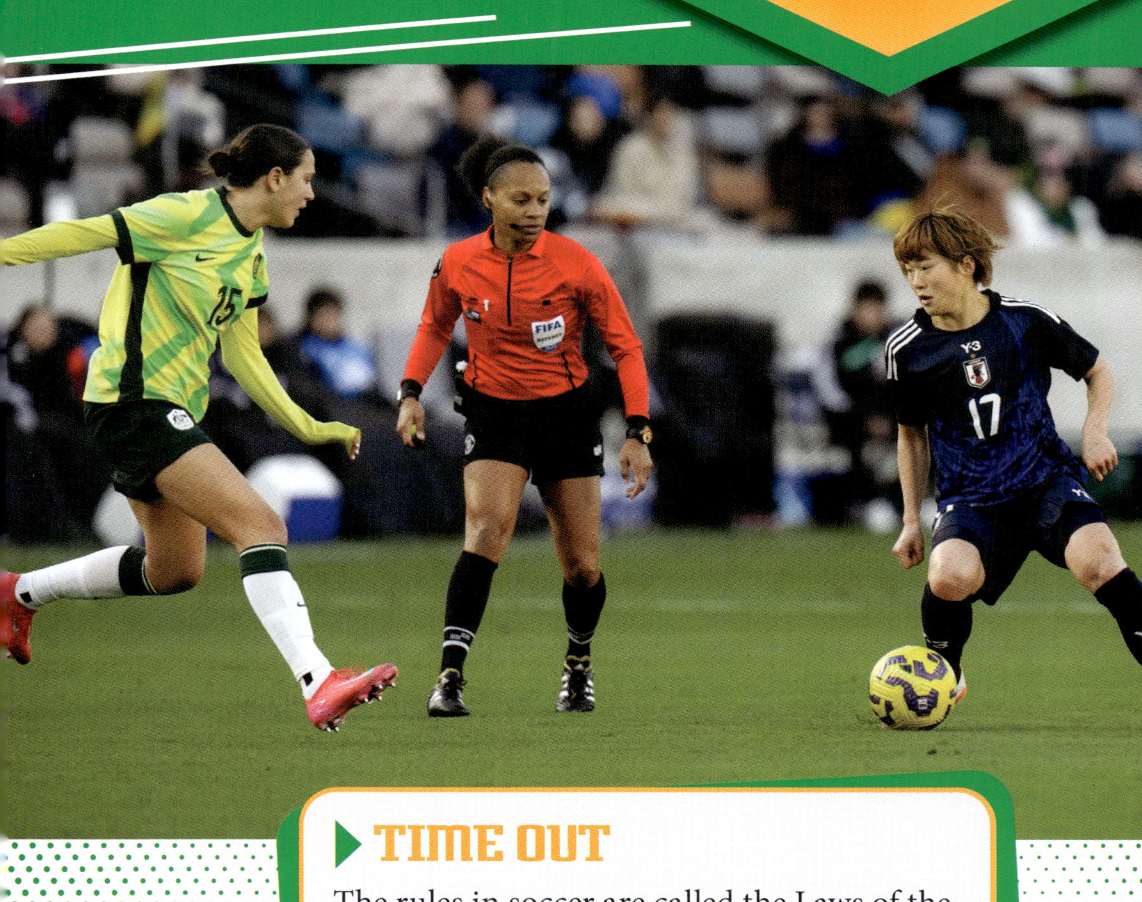

TIME OUT

The rules in soccer are called the Laws of the Game. They were established in 1897.

CHAPTER 1

OFFICIALLY IN CHARGE

While players run, pass, shoot, and score, officials also have a place in the action. During a professional soccer match, officials are responsible for making sure everyone plays by the rules. It's the only way to have a fair game.

In professional soccer, the officials include a head referee who's in charge of rules relating to game play, time on the clock, ball requirements, and penalties. He or she also stops the match if a player is hurt.

Two assistant referees, sometimes known as linesmen, help the head ref. They stand at the **touch lines**, so they're well positioned to make calls when the ball is out of bounds and **offside**.

Officials have some serious responsibilities when they're on the soccer field. Referees wear uniforms and a whistle. They use special flags, cards, and hand signals when they make their calls. They flip the coin that determines which team attacks first. They have a lot of power during a match, and they've earned it.

Referees don't just jump into officiating professional games. They take courses to learn the rules of soccer. They start out at local, regional, and national level games. As they learn more, they work their way up to officiating at pro soccer matches.

TIME OUT

As of 2025, professional soccer referees earn about $17.66 per hour in the United States. It's part-time work many people enjoy for the love of the game.

Officials keep a close eye on the match. But they don't have to just rely on their own vision to make the right calls. They use technology to capture and review plays on camera with video assistant referees (VARs).

VARs replay recordings within seconds to see different perspectives and double-check what happened. And they keep in contact with officials on the pitch to **confirm** and question the referees' decisions.

But even with training, education, and VAR, officials will still make controversial calls. Read on for three epic moments involving controversial calls and put yourself on the pitch.

COULD YOU HANDLE THE PRESSURE OF BEING A REF?

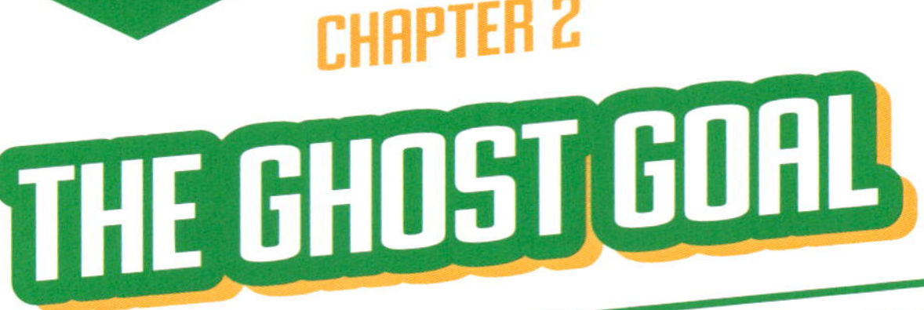

CHAPTER 2

THE GHOST GOAL

In 2010, England and Germany played in a FIFA World Cup match that seemed to be heading in Germany's favor. They were up 2–1 in the thirty-eighth minute. England's Frank Lampard aimed to change that.

Fans watched as Lampard took a shot that sent the ball sailing toward the goal. German goalkeeper Manuel Neuer stretched his arm upward, but the ball flew over his hand. The ball hit the underside of the crossbar and continued into the goal. It bounced on the ground, well over the line. The crowd went wild! The game was now tied!

BUT WHAT HAPPENED NEXT SHOCKED EVERYONE.

Officials didn't call a goal for England! Fans, players, and commentators were outraged. How did the officials not see what everyone else saw?

THE BALL CLEARLY CROSSED THE LINE BY TWO TO THREE FEET!

But officials missed the moment. An assistant referee was 15 yards away. The head referee was even farther away and distracted by other action on the field. Lampard's effort became known as a ghost goal—a legitimate goal that wasn't awarded. The game continued, as it always does. In the end, Germany won with a score of 4–1.

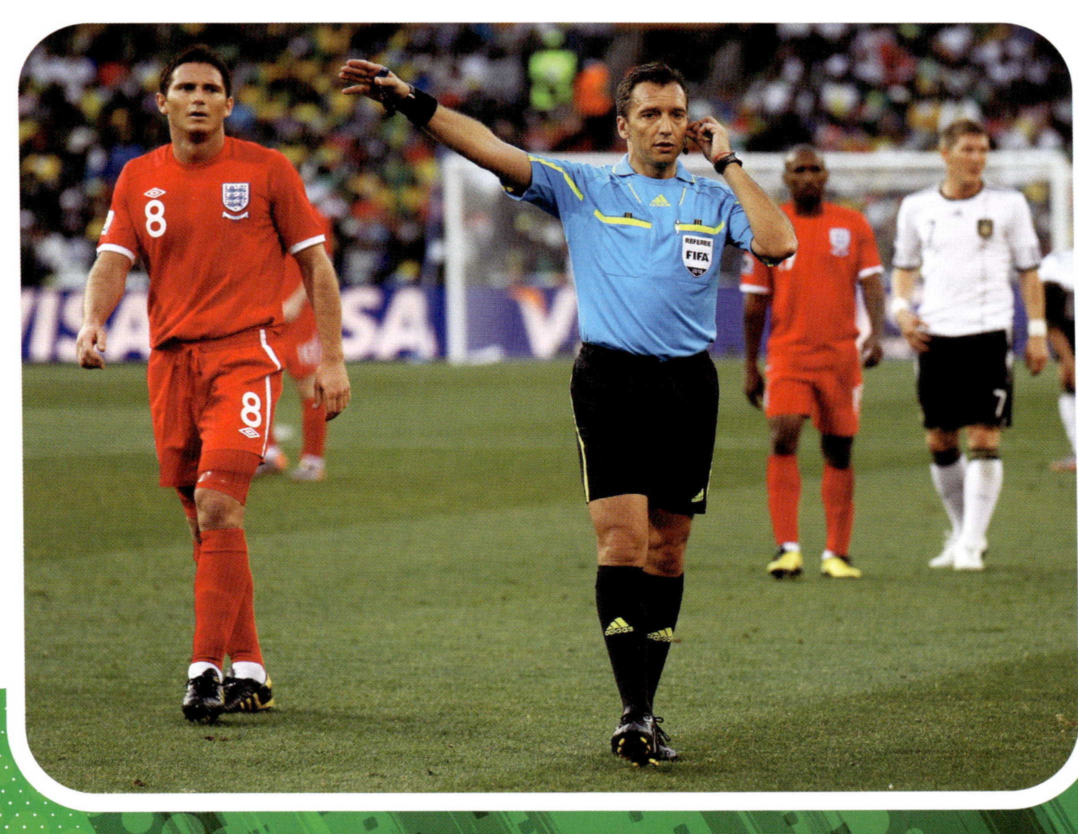

After the game, officials admitted the error. But it was too late to change the outcome of the match.

"It was a very fast shot that I did not see properly, even though I was located in the right place," assistant referee Mauricio Espinosa said later.

TIME OUT

The FIFA World Cup is an international tournament that pits teams from all over the world against each other. It takes place every four years.

You're called up as an assistant referee.

Frank Lampard's shot flies toward the German goal. It hits the crossbar and continues into the net.

The ball bounces on the ground. You're far away and distracted by other action on the field.

Were you able to see when and where the ball landed? Can you confirm the goal?

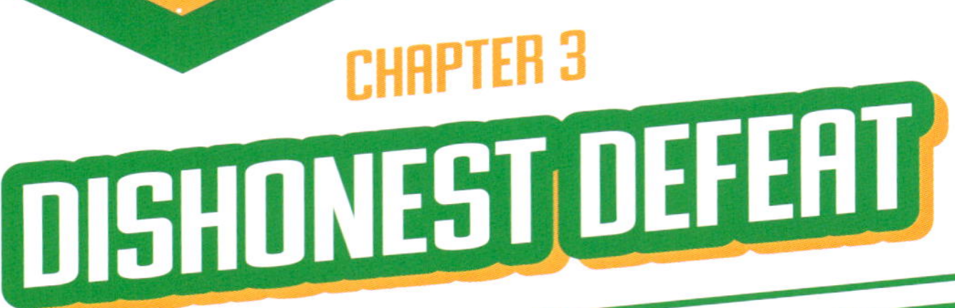

CHAPTER 3

DISHONEST DEFEAT

As halftime approached during the 1986 FIFA World Cup match between England and Argentina, neither team had a clear path to victory. Forty-five minutes into the game, no one had scored a goal.

At the start of the second half, however, a pass sent the ball high into the air. It was near Argentinian player Diego Maradona and English goalkeeper Peter Shilton. Shilton was much taller, but Maradona had an idea. He jumped up with his hand **outstretched** near his head.

TIME OUT

Peter Shilton holds the record for playing 1,387 professional soccer games, more than any other player in history.

WHAT HAPPENED NEXT?

The ball hit his hand, and he punched it into the goal! Maradona had used his hand to make the goal. That's a clear **violation** of the rules. However, the officials missed it! They confirmed the goal.

Maradona and his teammates celebrated. Argentina went on to win the match against England. The final score was 2–1. After the game, Maradona had all kinds of excuses about what had happened. He told reporters his head hit the ball. He also claimed the ball bounced off Shilton into the goal. He even said a higher power had intervened.

PEOPLE STARTED CALLING THE PLAY THE "HAND OF GOD."

Argentina continued playing in the World Cup. By the end of the tournament, they claimed the trophy. But how fair was the win? Photos proved officials made the wrong call in the match against England. Maradona used his hand to score the controversial goal. Years later, he admitted it. But that didn't change what happened in 1986.

You have replaced the head referee.

A high pass moves toward Diego Maradona. He jumps up with his hand outstretched near his head.

He punches the ball past goalkeeper Peter Shilton.

But did Maradona use his hand to score the goal? If so, it shouldn't count. Do you confirm the goal or not?

CHAPTER 4

TECH-ASSISTED TRIUMPH

In the 2023 FIFA Women's World Cup, Sweden and the U.S. were well matched. After 120 minutes of play, neither team had scored a goal. The game was almost over, but Sweden was about to take a **penalty** kick.

The shot was Swedish player Lina Hurtig's to make or miss. She aimed and kicked the ball right at the goal. U.S. goalkeeper Alyssa Naeher was positioned, ready to block.

As the ball came toward her, Naeher reached for it, but couldn't hold on. It flew through her hands and landed at the goal line, where Naeher grabbed it and pulled it back.

When the play was over, everyone wondered: Did the ball cross the goal line first, or did Naeher get it first?

If the goal was confirmed, Sweden would pull ahead. But it was too close to call. Even the referees couldn't be sure about the goal. Officials called for a VAR review.

Naeher had no doubt she'd succeeded in saving the penalty. Technology told a different story. The shot made it in by mere millimeters. Officials gave Sweden the goal. Sweden won the game, and the U.S. was out of the tournament.

It was such a stunningly close call that Naeher still didn't believe it. Some of her teammates agreed the U.S. should have won the match. It seems **plausible** that a judgment based on millimeters could go one way or the other based on the perspective of the cameras.

BUT THE OFFICIALS HAVE THE FINAL SAY.

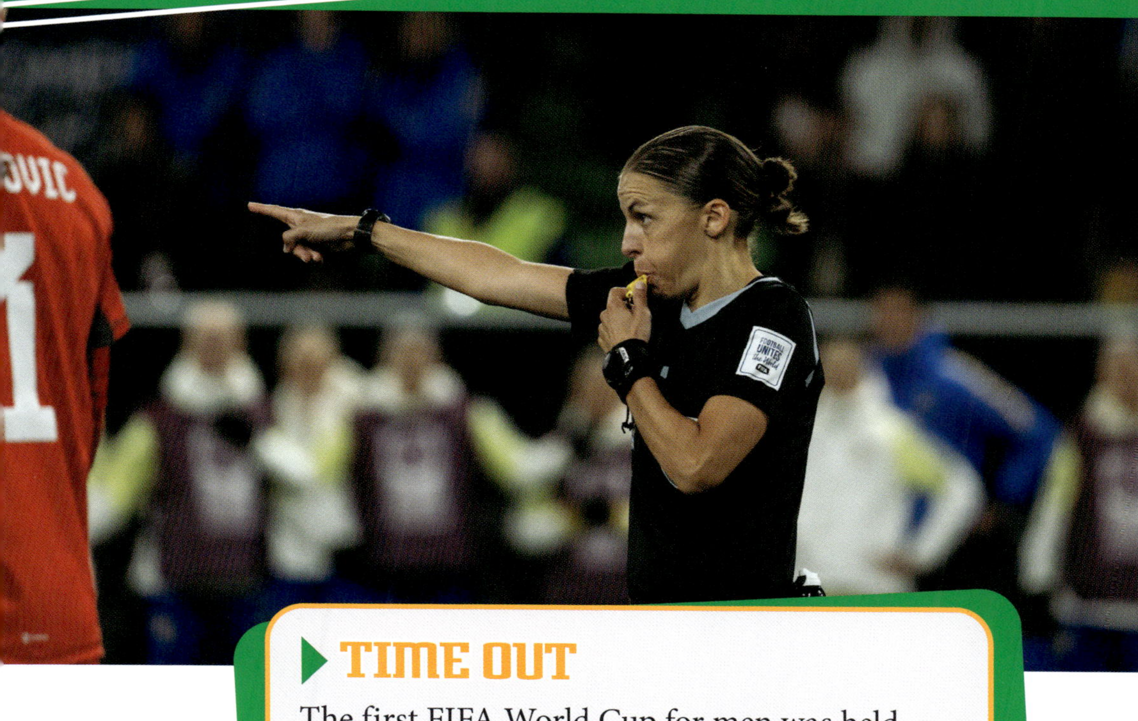

TIME OUT

The first FIFA World Cup for men was held in Uruguay in 1930. The first Women's World Cup took place in China in 1991.

You're the head referee.

Swedish player Lina Hurtig fires the ball toward the goal.

U.S. player Alyssa Naeher lunges to pull it back from the goal line.

Did Hurtig make the goal or not?

Do you use VAR or make the call without it?

Being a soccer official is a hard job. Players, coaches, and fans depend on officials to get calls right. But officials are just people. Sometimes their calls come down to an opinion about what happened on the field. Like anyone else, they make mistakes. Even calls backed up or overturned by VAR can cause controversy.

Do you have what it takes to be a professional soccer official?

COULD YOU MAKE THE CALL?

GLOSSARY

confirm (kuhn-FURM)—to uphold a decision

enforce (en-FORSS)—to put or keep rules in place

offside (AWF-sahyd)—in a position where the ball is not allowed

outstretch (out-STRECH)—to extend

penalty (PEN-uhl-tee)—a punishment for breaking the rules

plausible (PLAW-zuh-buhl)—having an appearance of truth

regulate (REG-yuh-layt)—direct by a rule

thwart (THWAWRT)—to prevent from happening

touch line (TUHCH LAHYN)—the long side of the field in soccer or rugby

violation (vahy-uh-LAY-shuhn)—a breach of the rules

READ MORE

Berglund, Bruce. *Soccer GOATs: The Greatest Athletes of All Time*. North Mankato, MN: Capstone Press, 2024.

Braun, Eric. *Goal: The Science Behind Soccer's Most Exciting Plays*. North Mankato, MN: Capstone Press, 2025.

Radnedge, Keir. *World Soccer Records 2025*. London: Welbeck, 2024.

INTERNET SITES

FIFA
fifa.com/en

Major League Soccer: How Do You Become an MLS Referee?
mlssoccer.com/news/how-do-you-become-mls-referee-process-grassroots-explained

U.S. Soccer: Referee Program
ussoccer.com/referee-program

INDEX

ABOUT THE AUTHOR

Heather E. Schwartz writes children's books on a wide variety of topics. She lives in upstate New York with her husband, two kids, and two cats.